The Basic Essentials of
SOLO CANOEING

by Cliff Jacobson

**Illustrations by
Cliff Moen**

ICS BOOKS, Inc.
Merrillville, Indiana

THE BASIC ESSENTIALS OF SOLO CANOEING

Copyright © 1991 by Cliff Jacobson

10 9 8 7 6 5 4 3 2 1

Printed in U.S.A.

DEDICATION

In memory of Sharon Kay Jacobson: 1940–1990. "She brightened every life she entered."

ACKNOWLEDGMENTS

A special thanks to Harry Roberts, Charlie Wilson, and John Winters, for their advice and contributions to this book.

Published by:
ICS Books, Inc.
One Tower Plaza
107 E. 89th Avenue
Merrillville, IN 46410

Library of Congress Cataloging-in-Publication Data

Jacobson, Cliff.
    The basic essentials of solo canoeing / by Cliff Jacobson.
        p.   cm. -- (Basic essentials series)
    Includes index.
    ISBN 0-934802-66-1 : $4.95
    1. Canoes and canoeing.   I. Title.
GV783.J28 1991
797.1'22--dc20   90-26010
                                               CIP

TABLE OF CONTENTS

8.19

PREFACE

On my 19th birthday, Dad gave me a well-used but immaculate pearl white 57 Plymouth. It had quad-headlights, balloon whitewalls, a push-button tranny, and two ominous dorsal fins.

I never let on I hated the car!

Three months later, I replaced the Plymouth with an ebony black vintage MG. The throaty roar, red leather upholstery, and chrome wire wheels, suggested it was a "real driving machine." Dad wasn't impressed. He called the MG a "selfish man's car." "No room for your friends," he admonished.

No matter. The MG was *fun* to drive and that was reason enough to buy it.

Shortly thereafter, I became interested in canoes. First I bought a tubby Royalex boat, then a stoic aluminum one. Ultimately, I graduated to sweet, lithe cruisers which were artfully constructed from fiberglass, Kevlar, and polished wood.

Dad never understood my love of sports cars, but he did appreciate canoes. Too bad he never had the opportunity to paddle a solo canoe. I think he'd have liked these "selfish man's" boats.

What's with the revival of interest in solo canoes? I say "revival" for one person boats are nothing new. Check out your history books. Indian bark canoes were typically small—15 feet or so, and commonly

i

paddled alone. The Eskimo kayak was a solitary craft too, though occasionally, an ambitious Inuit might sneak the kids into the craft for short trips. Sure, there were war canoes and umiacs and bull boats, but primitive man preferred to paddle alone.

Late nineteenth century Americans embraced the solo canoe with joy and gusto. Big canoes were for work. Little ones were for play. It was this philosophy that earned Henry Rushton a fluorishing business building ultra-light* "personal canoes" in the 1890's. Indeed, it wasn't until well into the 20th century that the efficiency of "doing it together" obsoleted the joy of going alone.

But that's old hat now, for Americans are again re-discovering the pleasures of the solo canoe—of being able to go paddling on a whim, when and where they want, and with no arguments from a reluctant partner.

If there's water enough to float a toy sailboat, there's water enough for soloing. You don't need a raging river, classifiable rapid, or tireless expanse of open water to have a good time. Paddling *your way* at your own pace on the water of your choosing is what solo canoes are all about.

---

* The Sairy Gamp was the lightest of Rushton's canoes. At nine feet long with a beam of 26 inches, it weighed a scant ten and one-half pounds. Sairy Gamp was a lapstrake canoe built of three-sixteenths inch cedar. No glues of any type were used in its construction.

1. LIKE A YELLOW LEAF IN AUTUMN

I discovered the solo canoe on a gentle river in central Minnesota. It was 1973, before the dawn of the solo canoe revolution. In those days, if you wanted to paddle alone, you tricked out a narrow tandem canoe with a center seat and knee pads and pretended the boat was built for one. If you desired a pure-bred solo cruiser you had to build your own, maybe even design it.

Using plans from the Minnesota Canoe Association* and heavy help from friend and nationally known canoe designer, Bob Brown, I built my first cedar-strip solo canoe (the MCA 14-footer). The gentle 14-footer was grand for spooning the quiet ponds near home, but it was too slow and unseaworthy for the big lakes and bouncy rivers I loved to paddle.

So back to the drawing board we went. A solo boat should feel stable at rest and when leaned to the rails; it should have good speed and paddle easily, carry a moderate load without balking, and be seaworthy enough to negotiate moderate rapids and running waves with a week's load of camping gear aboard. It should also be

---

* You can get a variety of plans for building wood-strip solo and tandem canoes from the MCA. Their canoe building book leaves nothing to chance. Members also get HUT magazine—a monthly publication for serious paddlers. The MCA is an all-volunteer organization, with members in all of the 50 states. Address: Minnesota Canoe Association, P.O. Box 13567, Dinkeytown Station, Minneapolis, MN 55414.

1

Figure 1-1. "Solo canoes. They set you free to follow your own star in your own way."

undeniably fun to paddle. What I wanted was a Canadian backwoods cruiser that could double as a sporty pleasure boat around home. I'd be satisfied with nothing less!

Nearly twenty years and dozens of prototypes later, I'm still searching for my "do everything" canoe. In my garage are three "little pointy boats"—plus the dream of owning a dozen more. As you'll discover, the solo bug bites deep: its venom may numb your love of tandem canoes as you succumb to the magic of paddling alone.

But the *solo canoe* is not just for solitary purists: it's for everyone who feels deeply the rhythms of nature and marvels at her beauty. It is for fishermen and hunters, for wildlife lovers, photographers, birders— all who need a sturdy craft to carry them across the water to places wild and free.

And it is for those special times when you want to be alone—like after work or at the end of a wilderness day when the light begins to fade. That's the time to go—to fish, to sit, or just to paddle.

Or maybe after weeks of planning a backwoods trip, your canoeing partner backs out. There's a three-some and you're odd man up. Aren't you glad you own a solo canoe?

If absolute speed is your game, read no further, for there's no way any solo canoe can be driven as fast as the best tandem boats. Merely a matter of physics: with just one engine churning, you'll naturally work harder than if you had a friend to help you keep up speed. Add a second paddler and you double the power. The more engines you run, the faster you go. The relationship only falters when you overload the boat. It's no mystery why the ungainly—by todays standards—ten man trade canoes of the Voyageurs were so quick.

Numbers tell only part of the story. A lone canoeist lacks the symmetry of a partner and the efficiency of the double blades of a kayak, so you go slower on the flats than a good team in a double boat, and much slower in a headwind. Nonetheless, you don't need to be a marathon champion to cover the miles rapidly or even to keep pace with your tandem friends. The *solo art* is easily mastered by anyone who understands the ways of the traditional Canadian canoe.

Paddling three or four strokes to the side on flat water with a bent shaft paddle of 54 inches or so, keeps the boat tracking and maximizes the flow of energy. As Harry Roberts will explain in chapter 7, even a rank beginner can solo efficiently for long periods of time by switching sides to maintain the course. And the traditional C-stroke of the soloist (see chapter 5), though essential for whitewater, is just too inefficient and tiring when used without compromise over the long haul.

Once in the rapids and the situation livens. Now you're both bow and stern—prying, drawing, cross-drawing, ferrying to get into the correct channel, through the clear vee, over the ledge, into the eddy. You draw barely two inches of water with a week's load of camping gear aboard. The mistakes you make are your own. You can't blame your partner, your spouse, or your mother-in-law. A screw-up is a screw-up and the consequences of poor judgment or skill are appropriately rewarded. Success is measured in terms of "I" not "we!"

Man-eating waves ahead? Stay calm, you're in control. Your little canoe leans when you lean, slips aside willingly, goes on command. It rides the biggest waves, the largest rapids, "like a yellow leaf in autumn." You use the rocker in the sidewall to spin the craft nearly broadside to the largest waves, tilting the hull to gain needed freeboard. Once through the pitch, a gentle flick of your paddle aligns the boat with the current.

Attach your fabric cover and plunge confidently ahead through the biggest stuff. So what if the bow buries in a fluorish of foam? Your nylon cover keeps you dry. Rock ahead? Draw! Hard...again and again. Blend to a diagonal draw astern and set gently ashore or into a quiet eddy to await the arrival of your friends in their tandem canoes.

Ahead, beyond the shallows, nested in a maze of boulders is the portage trail. Can your friends in their bulky two man boats get there without scraping, banging, thumping, hanging up, getting out, walking, wading...cussing?

No. But you can!

Fifty yards up the hill is the start of the carry. But getting there requires scrambling over pillows of rock which are half submerged in a sticky sea of black mud. You test the surface of the mud with your paddle. The blade sinks quietly out-of-sight. There's time enough to pick a route—your friends are still struggling at the mouth of the channel.

First, unload the canoe. Grab the big pack and both paddles, then pick your way meticulously over the rocks towards the beckoning portage. You drop the gear next to a small black spruce at the start of the trail, then unencumbered, scramble back to your awaiting canoe.

The big boats have nearly arrived and already there is a pandemonium of confusion. You don't want your finely crafted solo canoe to get mashed between these monsters. Better work fast!

Deftly, you swing the little day pack to your shoulders, lift a near gunnel of your canoe, and suitcase-style, carry the boat a few yards to a level spot where you can attach the contoured wood yoke and make a proper carry.

The boulders and muck are behind you now, but the tandem teams are in hot pursuit. Your pace quickens. Overhead are frequent wood-framed canoe rests built by the Forest Service, but there's no need to use them. After all, you can easily carry your 38 pound canoe and light pack the full mile distance without stopping. A smug smile flashes briefly. You may have puffed along energetically in the hind quarter on that windy ten mile lake, but now you're leading the pack with a lighthearted spirit that your more "sociable" friends can only marvel at.

To you, the portage is a delightful mixture of gentle sounds, lucious green forest, and dampled vegetation. To your friends, it is an ominous sweaty encumberence to be despised and disposed of as quickly as possible.

These are the joys of the solo canoe—joys that become more intense as the years creep by and suddenly you discover you're not as athletic as you used to be. Small-framed men and women need no introduction to the pleasures of soloing for they, more than anyone, understand what it means to be always last on the portage trail and forever chained to the bow seat of a tandem canoe.

Whitewater, flatwater, or local streams. The solo canoe will go anywhere a tandem canoe will go—a bit more slowly perhaps, but with a grace, style and elegance that is unmatched by any other watercraft.

Solo canoes. They set you free to follow your own star in your own way.

2. CHOOSING A SOLO CANOE

Figure 2-1. Choosing a solo canoe

There are short, bulky canoes for whitewater slalom; long, narrow ones for fast cruising and downriver racing; compact sportsters for messing around on mill ponds; high volume craft for wilderness tripping; rudder-equipped, decked models for ocean touring, and utility boats for fishing. And bridging these gaps are special purpose designs which accentuate one variable at the expense of another.

6

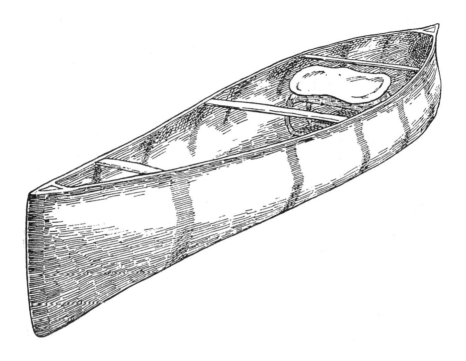

Figure 2-2. Flatwater racing canoe

Here's a summary of the differences:

Flatwater Racing Canoes

Length averages 17-18 feet, width at the gunnels around 24 inches, depth 12 inches, and weight, under 30 pounds. The sides are curved sharply inward (tumblehome) to reduce paddle reach. The pilot sits on a low-mounted sliding bucket seat and braces his feet firmly against a metal foot bar which is pop-riveted to the hull. Competitive race boats are built exclusively of Kevlar and closed-cell foam or an exotic combination of these and other high-tech materials. They feel stable at rest but will unhorse you instantly in rough water if you don't understand their ways.

Downriver Racers

Nearly identical to the canoes mentioned above, only with higher (14-15 inch) sides to keep out splash—a feature which increases seaworthiness but makes them wind-susceptible. The forte of these canoes is charging hell-bent-for-leather through rapids, which is all they do well.

Decked Whitewater Slalom Canoes

These look like kayaks, but they're wider and deeper, and you kneel on a pedestal or fitted ethafoam horse. Knee cups and toe blocks secure your position.

Why choose a decked slalom canoe over a kayak? First, you can exit faster in a capsize because you don't have to extract outstretched legs from the narrow confines of the hull. If a kayak deck is crushed by water pressure as the boat "wraps" around a boulder, there may be no getting out! The kneeling position also provides better visibility in rapids—the reason why kyakers often *follow* canoes through complex drops. However, slalom canoes are much slower than kayaks. And kneeling for very long is an exercise in misery.

Open Whitewater Play Boats

These low volume open canoes are great for playing in moderate rapids. Since there's no enclosed deck, you simply fall out of the boat if it capsizes—a very safe arrangement.

Length is 13-14 feet, depth 14-15 inches, width, around 30 inches. Construction is Royalex or Kevlar. Whitewater play boats usually have thwarts forward and aft, but no seat. You install an ethafoam saddle or bench seat, knee pads and toe blocks. These canoes are lively and turn on a dime, but like their decked cousins, they are difficult to paddle straight.

Freestyle Canoes

These intensely beautiful canoes are designed for the gentle art of messing around on quiet water. Their narrow waterlines produce a tippy feeling when sitting still, but the fully flared sides (no tumblehome) make these craft more stable when leaned. This design enables the paddler to "lay down" the hull to the rails when maneuvering, without shipping water or capsizing. Freestyle canoes are typically 12–13 feet long and 26–30 inches wide. Construction is ultralight fiberglass or Kevlar composite. For dynamic performance and stability, you *kneel* in these canoes!

Cruising Canoes

These are best described as "high performance do everything" canoes. They're fast on the flats, though not blistering so; they'll handle a wind-tossed lake or scary rapid with reasonable aplomb, and they'll twist easily through a complex rock garden, if you do your part. They're decidedly lively on all types of water, yet surprisingly forgiving when pushed to their limits.

Some cruising designs accentuate speed while others emphasize maneuverability or carrying capacity. Generally, ultrafast "sit'n switch" boats like the Sawyer Summersong and DY Special are best paddled from a low-seated, racing position with short, bent-shaft paddle. Steering is accomplished by switching sides every three strokes or so.

More general purpose craft, like the Mad River Slipper, Curtis Vagabond, and Bell Traveler, feature high-mounted (or adjustable) bench seats which provide the option of sitting or kneeling.

Then, there are the high volume backcountry cruisers which are built for big people or big loads. Length is standardized at around 15 1/2 feet, depth 12 inches, width at the rails, 28-30 inches. These canoes have gentle vee or shallow arch bottoms with moderate tumblehome amidships and substantial flare at each end to encourage seaworthiness. Canoes which best characterize this breed are the Bell CJ Solo (designed by Bob Brown and myself), Blackhawk Starship, and Curtis Nomad. These impeccably built cruisers will easily accomodate a 200 pound paddler and a month's load of camping gear.

Decked Cruisers

Take a sea kayak, shorten it some, add more width and depth plus a touch of lift (rocker) at each end, cut a long open cockpit, and you have a "decked cruiser." The Verlen Kruger designed Sea Wind, Mad River Monark, and Sawyer Loon exemplify this type.

Decked cruisers have a foot-operated rudder, sliding tractor seat with vertical adjustment, and a rolled deck combing which will accept a fabric spray cover. Advantages over a sea kayak include a more comfortable higher seating position, more efficient gear storage, better portability (you can attach a yoke for a conventional overhead carry) and increased maneuverability.

Though impeccably constructed from state-of-the-art Kevlar composites, these canoes are heavy (45-65 pounds) and not much "fun" to paddle. But they are very fast and capable in waters that would be too rough for a traditional open canoe.

Utility Canoes

These are 34-36 inches wide, flat-bottomed and emminently stable for fishing or photographing. Most are 10-12 feet long and are constructed of fiberglass or Royalex. Utility canoes are slow, noisy, relatively lightweight and inexpensive. The Old Town "Pack" is the most popular utility canoe in production.

Points to Consider When Choosing a Solo Canoe

Note: there are exceptions to all these rules. Canoe design and construction is too complicated to reveal all in this small space. The bottom line is that you should *always* paddle a prospective canoe before you buy it!

1. The longer the canoe the faster it will run. *However*, speed and "ease-of-paddling" *are not* the same. A long canoe will have a higher cruising speed than a shorter one, but you'll put out more effort to attain it—a factor to weigh heavily if you're not into racing and just want to paddle a responsive canoe. Fourteen-and-one half feet is probably the best all-around length for a solo cruising canoe that will also be used for light freestyle maneuvers and whitewater.

2. Thirty inches at the rails is the maximum width for a true solo canoe. The narrower the waist, the easier the paddle reach.

3. For straight ahead power, sit in your canoe and use a short bent-shaft paddle. For executing fancy maneuvers, use a straight (or nearly straight) paddle and *kneel*. Not all solo canoes—especially those with tractor seats—provide the option for assuming both positions comfortably.

4. The lighter the solo canoe the faster it will accelerate and the more perky it will feel. A lithe, well-built cruiser will weigh under 38 pounds. Except for rock-bashing whitewater, 45 pounds is the absolute limit for a true solo canoe. Ultra-light, high-tech Kevlar composite boats are worth the hundreds of extra dollars they cost. Compare a 35 pound Kevlar canoe to an identical 45 pound fiberglass one and you'll see why.

5. You have more control in a solo canoe than in a tandem one, so you're less likely to hit rocks. And when you do hit them, your boat incurs much less damage because its mass is about half that of the

bigger boat. It follows that a solo canoe may be fabricated with less material than a tandem canoe, yet be as strong under typical field conditions. So unless you'll be paddling hair-raising whitewater or plan to trek to the arctic, choose the *lightest* canoe you can find. I've put hundreds of miles on fiberglass-covered, cedar-strip canoes in the wilds of Canada, and consider them plenty strong enough for tripping.

6. A solo canoe should be sized to fit *your* traveling weight (weight of paddler plus gear). Most novices select canoes which are too big: experts generally pick the smallest boat they can get by with, for the reasons stated in 1, 2, 4 and 5.

7. Listen to what the experts recommend but take their advice *only* after you have paddled their choices. Athletic skill and physical differences—such as torso length and distribution of body weight— may make a usually docile craft feel twitchy to some people. Your canoe should reflect *your* personality, not your friend's or some expert's.

3. TUNING YOUR CANOE FOR MAXIMUM PERFORMANCE

There's a notion that canoes are "right" as they come from the factory. Witness the number of paddlers who complain about seat height and placement but won't do a darn thing to alter an uncomfortable situation. Ditto for slippery canoe bottoms, a badly designed yoke—or no yoke at all—and tie-down (lining) holes in the wrong places. The locaton or omission of "canoe features" was not ordained by God. You should definitely change what doesn't work best!

Seats

There's nothing more uncomfortable than paddling a high-sided canoe from a low seating position. Even if the canoe is arrow thin at the rails, you still wind up with the dreadful experience of paddling with a gunnel in your armpit.

The solution is to raise the seat (a half inch per practice session is enough) as high as you can tolerate. Don't be surprised if, after a season's use, your seat is "jacked to the rails." Note: a compromise is in order when paddling a skittish race boat or full blown whitewater hull.

Sliding seats add weight and cost; they're bulky and reduce underseat leg room, and they are not as strong as a fixed seat. A slider is essential in a racing canoe when you want to make slight trim adjustments but have no gear to balance the boat. Otherwise, opt for a fixed seat and use a light day pack or water bottle to trim your canoe.

Tip: you'll kneel more comfortably if the front edge of your seat is located about five-eighths inches *lower* than the back edge.

Knee Pads

Knee pads should be *glued* into the canoe. To make them, cut four 10" x 12" rectangles from a three-eighths inch thick closed-cell EVA (ethyl-vinyl-acetate) foam sleeping pad—available at most camping shops. Contact cement (I prefer Weldwood) two rectangles together to get a three-quarter inch thickness. Apply the glue with a foam varnish brush. When dry, apply a second coat to the faces of the pads that will be joined. Trim pads with a straight edge and sharp knife then sand the edges to a pleasing shape with an orbital sander and 60 grit paper. For a smooth, custom look, *lightly* flame the sanded area with a butane blow-torch.

Tip: use three thicknesses of foam in the bilge (to wrap the bilge curve and provide security for wide-spread knees) and two thicknesses on the bottom. All your "glue work" should be underneath, where it can't be seen.

Lining Holes at Cutwater

You can rig a towing harness (see my book, *The New Wilderness Canoeing & Camping*), when the need arises, or simply install lining holes near the waterline. For a neat look, drill a quarter-inch diameter pilot hole all the way through the hull, then, enlarge it *from each side* with a 3/8" bit.

This accomplished, go to work with a rat-tail file until the hole will accept a length of one-half inch diameter PVC water pipe. Cut the

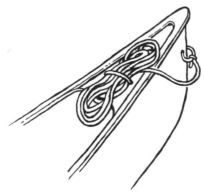

Figure 3-2a. Shockcord the deck.

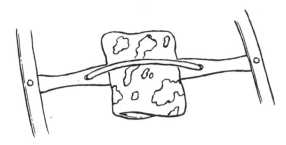

Figure 3-2b. A shockcorded thwart is a handy place to store your map.

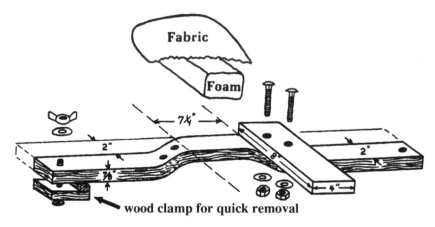

Figure 3-3. "A removeable yoke is essential, even for short carries."

pipe to fit and epoxy it into the hole. Chamfer the edges and spray paint to match the hull color. The resultant fitting is beautifully unobtrusive and as strong as the boat. Caution: don't attempt Mount Everest by initially drilling a one-half inch diameter hole. You'll chunk out pieces of gel-coat or skin covering. Better to drill undersize then enlarge by filing.

Shock-cord Your Thwarts and Decks (Figure 3-2a, b)

A backwoods touring canoe should have painters (tracking lines) at each end. Twenty feet of quarter inch polpropylene is enough. Coil each line carefully and store it under an elastic cord run through holes on the deck. This will secure it on portages and in a capsize, yet it will release instantly when pulled.

Tip: lengths of shock-cord strung through holes in the thwarts provide a handy place to store a light jacket or map.

Sponge

Every time you "HUT" (switch paddle sides), a few drops of water will spill into your canoe. After an hour's paddling, you'll want a sponge. Tie two loops of shock-cord around one arm of your seat frame and keep your sponge inside.

Yoke (Figure 3-3)

A removeable yoke is essential, even for short carries. Ash is the preferred wood, though it's stronger and heavier than you need for a 40 pound solo canoe. I saw my own yokes from three-quarter inch mahogany and finish them to the dimensions in Figure 3-3. Cushy foam-filled shoulder pads are a must no matter how light your canoe. Clamp wood or metal brackets to the gunnels with a bolt and giant wing-nut. Cement a piece of leather underneath the yoke bar at each end to prevent the yoke from slipping and/or marring the wood rails of your canoe.

Figure 3-4. Splash Cover

Nylon Splash Cover (Figure 3-4)

A *splash cover* will keep you dry in rain and rapids and cut wind resistance by at least half. It is your "edge" when nosing into waves in the company of heavier tandem canoes.

After years of experimenting, I've come to prefer a two piece model which I designed (Figure 3-4). The tail portion extends from the rear thwart to the deck plate. The front apron overlaps and Velcroes to the tail section, or it can be rolled and reefed just forward of the paddler or behind the deck plate when portaging. There is a quick-release gusset in the waist skirt for instant bail-out. The entire cover consumes two fistfuls of space and weighs just 30 ounces.

You'll find detailed plans for making a splash cover in my book *Canoeing Wild Rivers*, or you can get a commercial rendition of my design for the most popular boats from Sawtooth Mountain Sled Works, Inc. Rt. 3, Box 693, Grand Marais, MN 55604.

Whitewater Fittings

If you choose a full-blown whitewater canoe, you'll need to install an ethafoam kneeling saddle, knee pads, toe blocks, thigh straps, and float bags. It is beyond the scope of this book to consider the details of these fittings. You'll find specific information for "tuning" the whitewater solo canoe in these books: *Basic River Canoeing*, by McNair and Landry; *Solo Canoeing*, by John McPhee, *Whitewater; Quietwater*, by Bob and Jody Palzer.

4. PADDLES, PFD'S AND ACCESSORIES

Don't minimize the importance of top shelf accessories. A paddle must feel right to work right. Same with life jackets, packs, and the gamut of paddling gear. At the outset, go slowly on your purchases: a few high quality items are better than a shedful of mediocre stock. Listen to what the experts tell you but choose products which meet *your* paddling needs.

How to Pick a Paddle

There are *straight* paddles, bent paddles, and sexy looking S-blades with two and one-half degree offsets. For the ultimate in efficiency with dead quiet entry and no wasted power, some paddle blades have hydrodynamically curved tips which grab the water and sweep it directly into the scientifically shaped blade.

One piece wood paddles? There are a few around, mostly nostalgic ash beavertails and toys for the kids. Everything else is laminated from select wood and fiberglass, or carefully alloyed from E-glass, S-glass, Kevlar, graphite, closed-cell foam, and other synthetic materials. The new paddling sticks are lighter, stronger, and *more comfortable* to use than anything the Indians ever built. And they are far more beautiful too. If you think American craftsmanship went out with the great depression, you'd best hold your tongue until you've tried the state-of-the art paddling furniture.

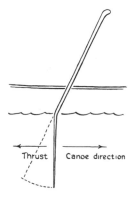

Figure 4-1. Why the bent paddle is more efficient.

Figure 4-2. S-blade paddle.

Choose a *straight* paddle if you're primarily interested in precision canoe *control*. Running technical whitewater and maneuvering around obstacles on a beaver pond, are both reasons to select a straight blade.

Bent-shaft paddles: A straight paddle lifts water at the end of a stroke and slows the canoe. A *bent* paddle pushes it *straight back*. Figure 4-1 shows why the bent shaft is more efficient.

Years of racing experience suggest that for going fast, nothing equals a 14-15 degree bent-shaft paddle. Lesser bends enhance control in the turns but are woefully inefficient on the flats. But with practice comes perfection: in time, you may even come to prefer your bent paddle for complex maneuvering.

The S-blade (figure 4-2) is *the* tool for executing the most graceful maneuvers on quiet water. S-blades feature custom-fitted rolled-over

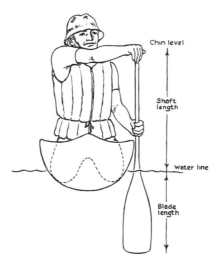

Chin level

Shaft length

Water line

Blade length

Figure 4-3. "Paddle shaft length equals the distance from your chin to the water."

(uni-directional) grips and curved tips. These paddles are very expensive and worth it!

Sizing Your Canoe Paddle

Two decades ago, solo canoeists were told to pick a paddle that came to their cycs. Then, in the early eighties, there came a revelation that the length of a paddler's *upper torso* (that part of your body above the canoe seat), was a better determinant of paddle length. Suddenly, the rules for paddle selection could be amended to read:

1. Set your canoe in the water and climb aboard.

2. Measure the distance from your chin (height of the top grip) to the water. That's the *shaft* length (Figure 4-3). To this add the length of the blade (20-25 inches, depending on paddle style). That's the correct paddle length. Note that the overall length of the paddle is largely programmed by the blade length.

To size a paddle *without* a canoe, stack up some books to equal the height of your canoe seat. Now, sit down and measure from the floor to your chin. This would be the correct shaft length if your canoe rode *on top* of the water. Now decrease the measured shaft length by an amount equal to the expected draft of your canoe. This figure should equal 2-3 inches for the typical solo touring boat, maybe an inch less for a pudgy whitewater craft. Bent paddles can be a bit shorter; whitewater sticks may be longer.

Paddle length is also a function of how you *choose* to paddle. Couple a fast cadence with a side switch ("HUT") every three strokes, and you'll want a short paddle. For carving effective turns, you'll want the extra reach of a long paddle.

Blade size: big blades are best for slow cadence maneuvers; small ones are better for fast, sit'n switch paddling.

Confused by the technicalities of paddle selection? A 56-58 inch straight paddle or a 53-55 inch 14º bent shaft, will get your solo cruising boat around the lake in fine style.

Paddle Bag

Protect your expensive paddle by transporting it to and from the river in a padded case. Buy a commercial model or make your own.

Life Jacket (PFD)

Your *Coast Guard approved* PFD should pass these tests:

Ride-up: Grasp the jacket by the shoulders and lift it upwards until the fabric jams under your armpits. This simulates performance in water. Now turn your head right and left. You should be looking *over* your shoulder, not at fabric-encased foam. Does the V-neck of the vest crunch against your chin? If so, keep shopping!

Arm function: Take a seat. This test won't work while standing or kneeling. Now, work your arms vigorously in a paddling motion. Reject any vest which chafes under the armpits.

flexibility: Hold your arms chest high and draw them smartly inward as far as possible. Does the vest bunch up in front and cramp arm motion? If so, don't buy it!

It should go without saying that your PFD should be worn *at all times*!

Thwart Bag

These handy bags attach to a canoe thwart or seat frame and provide ready access to camera, bug dope, and other frequently used essentials. Some designs Velcro shut; others have zippers or roll and buckle closures. Choose a style that you can access quickly with *one* hand.

Day Pack

You need a small day pack of some sort in which to keep rain gear, sweater, maps, first-aid kit, etc. A simple, frameless hiking pack is ideal.

5. The Paddler's Art

On rare occasions, I'm treated to the luxury of sharing my tandem canoe with someone who is experienced in the solo art. I say "luxury," because solo proficiency usually spells superior performance in the bow or stern of a double canoe. In fact, I can't think of a better way to improve tandem paddling skills than to frequently paddle alone.

In this chapter, we'll examine the paddle strokes which are unique to the solo canoe. Be prepared for some "upsetting experiences" as you learn, but don't let these dampen your enthusiasm for soloing. Like skating and water-skiing, "tipping over" is part of the learning curve.

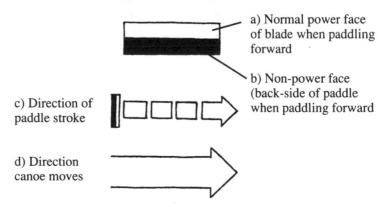

a) Normal power face of blade when paddling forward

b) Non-power face (back-side of paddle when paddling forward

c) Direction of paddle stroke

d) Direction canoe moves

Figure 5-1. Diagrams in this book will use this identificatiion system.

Figure 5-2. Solo-C   **Figure 5-3.** Sugar Island blade style

Read and practice. Observe good paddlers. Join a canoe club and attend on-water symposiums. In no time, you'll be duplicating the maneuvers outlined by Harry Roberts and Charlie Wilson. And in your quest for mastery, you'll enjoy a whopping good time!

Going Forward

First order of business is to learn to paddle your canoe in a straight line. You can "solo-C" or "sit'n switch," or alternate between the two. The competent soloist is expert at both methods.

The Solo-C

Tools: learning will come easier if you select a well-balanced, relatively long (56"-60") straight paddle, with an 8 - 8 1/2 inch wide Sugar Island style blade (figure 5-3). Blade corners should be smoothly rounded and edges ground wafer-thin. Save your 14 degree bent-shaft for making time on the flats or until you understand the mechanics of the straight paddle.

Begin the *solo-C* by reaching *comfortably* forward, power face of the paddle at a 30-45 degree angle to the canoe (figure 5-2). Arc the blade powerfully inward, curving the blade smoothly *under* the bilge of the canoe. Finish with a *smooth* outward thrust to correct your course. The stroke is executed in one fluid motion. If done correctly, the bow of your canoe will barely waver.

Points to remember: start turning the thumb of your top hand down and away from your body at the *very start* of the stroke. Progressively increase the pitch of the blade—and downward turn of your thumb—as the paddle is pulled through the water. At stroke's end, the thumb of your top hand should be pointing straight down as you go into the final outward push. Some of the best free-style canoeists hold the grip of the paddle at an angle to make the stroke more fluid.

Learn the mechanics of turning your top thumb down while gradually increasing the blade pitch, and you'll have the stroke down pat. A relaxed, straight-line run tells you you're doing it right.

"Hut Stroke" or "Minnesota Switch"

In the 1940's, two Minnesoteans—Tom Estes and Eugene Jensen—adopted an unusual procedure for keeping a racing canoe on course. After a half dozen strokes or so, the stern person would call "HUT," and the pair would switch paddling sides. This eliminated the need for the correctional J-stroke, which wasted power. Over the years, the *Minnesota Switch* or *HUT* stroke grew in popularity, and today, all professional canoe racers and fast cruisers use it.

To an old school canoeist, the *Minnesota switch* is an example of poor technique, largely because the canoe does not run arrow-straight. But the stroke is efficient, especially when you need to make time across a wind-swept lake.

Procedure: sit low in the canoe with feet braced (foot braces are higly desirable) firmly ahead. As the canoe begins to veer, switch sides. Two to three strokes per side is par for most solo cruising canoes. If you HUT correctly, only a split second is lost. If you fumble in a strong current, a capsize is possible.

Tools: you'll want a short (51"-54"), ultralight, 14 degree bent paddle. Many soloists prefer a one or two inch longer paddle shaft than they use in their tandem canoes. Harry Roberts will teach you the fine points of sit'n switch canoeing in chapter 7.

The Reverse-C

The *reverse-C* is used for backing the solo canoe in a straight line. Except for a bit more thrust and lag time near the end of the stroke, it is the exact opposite of the *forward-C* illustrated on page 22. Whitewater canoeists routinely pry the paddle shaft off the gunnel to straighten the canoe, but freestyle paddlers wouldn't dream of abusing their expensive paddles in this manner.

Sweeps

Use the forward sweep for making a gentle *off-side* (away from

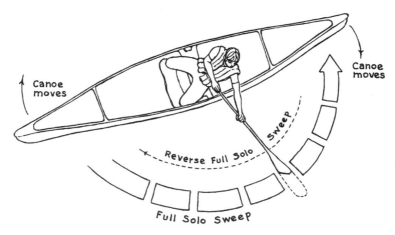

Figure 5-4. Solo Sweep

your paddle) turn. The *reverse sweep* turns you the other way. For more powerful turns, learn the *bow draw* (figure 5-5) and *cross-draw* (figure 5-7).

Figure 5-5. Bow Draw

Bow Draw

Essentially the first part of a *solo-C* stroke, but applied farther out and towards the bow. The *bow draw* is the fastest and most powerful way to turn the canoe towards your paddle side. It is especially useful in currents where it functions as a gentle brake, a sturdy brace, and a powerful turn, all in one. Combine the *bow draw* with a strong on-side (towards your paddle) lean and throw your shoulders into the stroke. The bracing action of your paddle will prevent the canoe from capsizing.

Like the *C-stroke*, the *bow draw* requires practice to master, mostly because of the awkward top hand position (the wrist is turned so the thumb is *down*—power face of the paddle faces the canoe). Keep your top arm *away* from your body and your hand almost on top of the grip, and the stroke will come naturally.

Figure 5-6. Draw Stroke

Draw Stroke

Use the *draw* to move your canoe laterally towards your paddle side. *Procedure*: reach out as far from the gunnel as you can. Keep your top hand high and *in front of your body** and draw the paddle quickly and powerfully inward. When the blade is within 6 inches of the canoe, slice it out of the water *towards the stern* and draw again. It's almost like a forward stroke done to the side.

Caution: when executing the *draw* in a tandem canoe, you customarily lean way out over the side and rely on the bracing effect of the matched *draws* to keep you from capsizing. In a tender solo canoe the lean is much less pronounced. This advice applies only to *calm* water: in cross-currents, you lean, brace, and draw, as the situation demands.

---

* This position is essential to prevent possible shoulder dislocation in the event the paddle strikes a rock or is whipped backwards by a strong current.

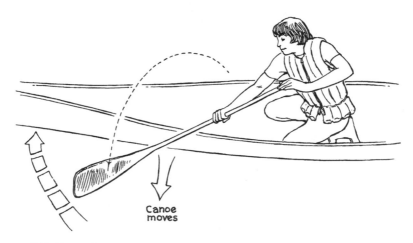

Canoe
moves

Figure 5-7. Cross-draw

Cross-Draw

This is the most powerful stroke for turning away from your paddling side, especially when the craft is under way. If strongly applied and coupled with a strong lean, it will snap even a straight-keeled solo canoe around in record time.

Procedure: pivot at the waist, swing the paddle over the boat, and *draw*! Don't change your grip on the shaft. Angle the paddle forward so that it is nearly parallel to the water, then force water *under* the boat, using the same power face as the *draw*. For greatest leverage, apply the stroke as close to the bow as possible.

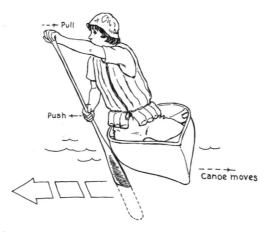

Figure 5-8. Pry Stroke

Pry (Figure 5-8)

The *pry* moves the canoe sidways, away from your paddle side. It is best at home in heavy water (powerful waves) where you need a quick lateral move plus the stability (bracing action) of a paddle that's always in the water.

However, the *pry* chews up paddle shafts and gunnels—the reason why most solo canoeists avoid it. The alternative is to switch sides and *draw*, or to *cross-draw* with a strong diagonal component astern. For maneuvering in heavy whitewater, the *pry* has no peer. Otherwise, the alternatives work as well and are easier on equipment.

Procedure: keep your weight *centered* as you slice the paddle, blade parallel to the keel-line, as far under the canoe as possible. With a deft, powerful motion, pry the paddle over the bilge. When the paddle is just beyond *vertical*, stop, and rotate the paddle shaft 90 degrees *away* from your body until the blade is perpendicular (normal traveling position) to the canoe. Slice the blade back under the bilge, pivot the paddle shaft to the starting position, and execute another *pry*.

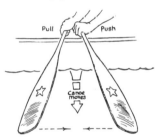

Figure 5-9. Sculling Draw

Sculling Draw

Use the *sculling draw* to move the canoe sideways in water that is too shallow to effect a good *draw*. Since there is no recovery phase, the *sculling draw* provides continous bracing action for the canoe—a plus when moving across currents.

Procedure: place the paddle in a *draw* position at a comfortable distance from the canoe. Turn the leading edge of the paddle about 45 degrees away from the canoe, and hold this angle as you pull the paddle straight backwards about two feet. Then reverse the angle of the blade 90 dgrees and, while holding this new blade angle, push the paddle back to its starting point.

Reverse Scull

The *reverse scull* moves the canoe *away* from your paddling side. It is the exact opposite of the *forward scull*, except that it is done very close to the canoe. A handy stroke on flat water, the *reverse scull* provides little bracing action in currents.

Figure 5-10. Low Brace

Figure 5-11. High brace

The Braces

The *low brace* functions as an outrigger: its purpose is to stabilize the canoe in turns and to keep it from capsizing in waves.

Procedure: reach out, paddle laid nearly flat on the water, knuckles *down*. If the canoe is underway, raise the leading (forward) edge of the blade above the oncoming water. This will encourage the blade to plane over the surface rather than submarine. Put your weight *solidly* on the paddle—a half-hearted effort isn't good enough. If you're capsizing towards your paddle side, a powerful downward push will right you. The push should be lightning fast and smooth; don't "slap" the water with your paddle.

You can use the low brace on calm water too: Get up a head of steam, reach back about 30 degrees and brace hard, power face at a strong climbing angle to the water. The canoe will spin right around your paddle, in effect executing an inside wheelee or "static axle." Charlie Wilson will detail this maneuver for you in chapter 8.

Note: when using a bent-shaft paddle, you will need to reverse the blade (and your grip hand) in order to commit the power-face to the *low brace* position. If the *palm down* attitude of your top hand seems awkward, keep practicing. The alternative is to abandon your bent paddle for a straight shaft. Rolling the shaft over (termed the "palm roll") takes time, so stick with the recommended backface down position when you need a brace fast!

High brace (figure 5-11): use this when you need a strong brace, a draw, and a canoe lean all at once. Essentially, the *high brace* is simply a stationary draw with the power face of the paddle held against the current or at a strong climbing angle to it. The success of the stroke depends on speed—either paddling or current—and a strong lean to offset the pull of the moving water.

When you find yourself capsizing to your off-side (side opposite your paddle), reach far out on a high brace and put your weight and trust on your paddle. Perfect this stroke early: you can't run whitewater without it!

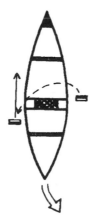

Figure 5-12. Cross Backstroke

Cross Back-stroke (Figure 5-12)

Use this when you need a powerful backstroke and a turn at the same time. It's similar to the *cross-draw*, only more severe. Rotate your shoulders and swing the paddle across the canoe. Then, execute a forward stroke with the normal power face of the paddle. By changing the angle of the paddle (add the components of the *reverse-C*), you can back the canoe dead straight. Or, you can go into a *cross-draw* for a fast turn to the off-side. The greatest value of the *cross back-stroke* is in rapids where you need reverse power on your "off" side. This is primarily a whitewater stroke: most cruising canoeists will never use it.

Leaning the Canoe

To make a gradual turn with the canoe *under power*, lean the hull (an inch or two is sufficient) to the *outside* of the turn (the reverse of what you would do on a bicycle). If you combine the lean with a *post* (see p. 41), the boat will spin right around your paddle. If you simply hold the lean (no *post*) while the canoe is at speed, it will cut a gentle arc in the *opposite* direction of the lean.

Blending Your Strokes

By now, you should realize that all solo maneuvers are essentially modifications of a few basic strokes. Learn the *draw* and *cross-draw*, the *sweeps*, and the *solo-C*, and the rest will come naturally. I had to separate strokes which I ordinarily combine in order to simplify them for you. Soloing is an exercise in fluid motion and combinations of stokes.

Soloing Your Tandem Canoe

Once you've experienced the magic of a pure-bred solo canoe, thoughts of single-handing a bulky tandem craft turn to yucch! After all, driving an 18-wheeler through a Grand Prix race course is no fun, even if you're adept at it. Nonetheless, if you do need to paddle your tandem boat alone, here's how:

Positions: the canoe should be trimmed *dead level*. Best procedure is to rig a removeable seat about 18 inches behind the center yoke bar. If you find it difficult to reach the water from your centralized position, scoot sideways and place both knees close together in the bilge of the canoe. This is a very comfortable position on quiet water, though you'll have to limit your paddling to one side.

Many people prefer to solo a tandem canoe from the stern seat because the canoe is so narrow at this point. But this knocks the canoe way out of trim. The bow rides high while the stern sinks low: in effect, you're paddling a seven-foot canoe with a ten-foot overhang. The slightest breeze will capsize you instantly. And any degree of control or speed is impossible.

All other "solo techniques"—paddling backwards from the bow seat, or stroking in the stern with the bow weighted, are inefficient and, to a greater or lesser extent, downright dangerous!

6. QUICK WATER MANEUVERS AND SAFETY CONCERNS

Even if you don't like whitewater, you should have a practiced command of the cross-stream ferry and eddy turn. These quick-water maneuvers will enable you to avoid rocks and fallen trees ("strainers") in a fast moving river.

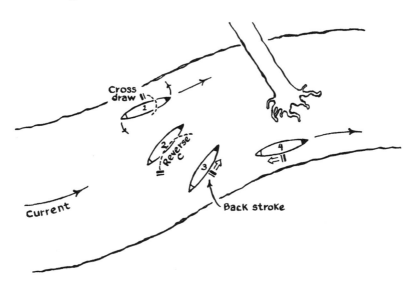

Figure 6-1. Backferry

The Cross Stream Ferry

Assume you're paddling on the right and an obstacle is dead ahead. Try to steer around it and you'll broadside for sure.

Instead, set up a *back ferry* as follows:

1. Use a powerful crossdraw to turn the canoe about 30 degrees to the current (figure 6-1). If you need more reverse power, blend to a *cross-backstroke*.

2. When the correct ferry angle is established, paddle backwards (*reverse-C*) on the downstream side. Maintain this angle and the canoe will scoot sideways, with no downstream slippage.

Tips: since you don't have the stabilizing effect of a partner, you may need to alternate between the *crossdraw*, *reverse-C*, and/or *reverse sweep*, to maintain directional control as you back the canoe. Things will go easier if you keep the downstream end of the canoe trimmed slightly *down* (shove your pack forward a foot or so before you begin the maneuver)

Another evasive tactic based on the principal of vectors is the *forward ferry*. It's identical to the back ferry except you spin the canoe 180 degrees to the current and paddle forward. Use the more powerful *forward ferry* to cross a wide river, a strong current, and whenever there is time to turn upstream.

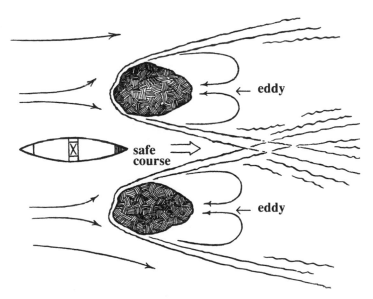

Figure 6-2. The eddy—a safe resting place in rapids

The Eddy Turn

Whenever water flows around an exposed rock, or the inside of a tight bend, an upstream current or *eddy* (figure 6-2) is formed. Eddies provide a convenient resting place from the rush of the current—that is, if you know how to cross the "eddy line."

Scenario: you're paddling on the right and want to enter the eddy on your left (figure 6-3a). Drive powerfully forward, blending to a sweep to turn the canoe. As the bow crosses the eddy line, go into a braced *crossdraw* (figure 6-3b) and lean the canoe sharply upstream (or "down-current" in relation to the actual flow). The canoe will spin around your paddle, into the quiet safety of the eddy.

If you are paddling on the *left*, drive forward as before, strongly *C-stroking* or switching sides as necessary to accelerate into the turn. As the bow crosses the eddy line, lean left and administer a stationary *bow draw* (hanging, open-faced high brace) on the port side of the canoe. For a more cautious entry, keep the canoe level and *backferry* into the eddy.

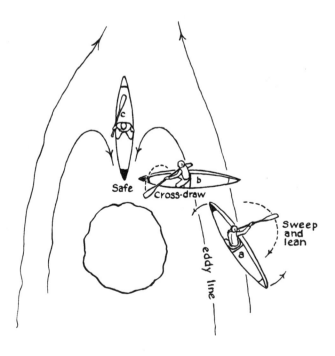

Figure 6-3. Eddy turn to the left

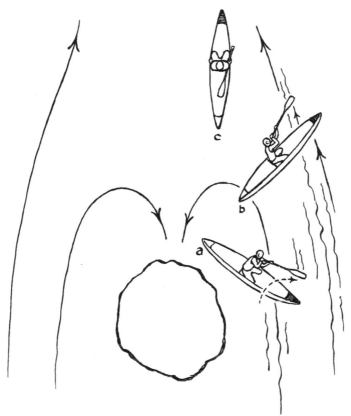

Figure 6-4. Complete eddy turn with braced cross draw on left.

To leave the eddy (if your paddle is on the right side): angle the canoe about 45 degrees to the river as you drive forward across the eddy line (figure 6-4). Lean *strongly* downstream and brace with a stationary *crossdraw*. Or...switch sides just before you cross the eddy line, then high-brace downstream.

Space does not permit a thorough treatment of whitewater procedures. Read the technique books listed at the end of this chapter if you want to learn more.

Safety Concerns

Capsizing on open water is your only real concern. Without a support crew, you'll have to swim your outfit to shore—reason enough to *always* wear a life jacket. Be sure your canoe has sufficient flotation so it won't sink. Flotation foam adds three or four pounds to a typical solo canoe, so minimal amounts are often used on high-performance craft.

Equip the ends of your canoe with "grab loops" or 12-foot lines, so you'll have something to hold as you drag the boat behind. Secure all gear into the canoe so it won't flop out in a capsize, and *always* "tie up" and/or invert the canoe whenever you land. Carry a knife, waterproof matches, whistle and first-aid kit, even if you're out for only a short time.

Note: getting water out of a solo canoe that's swamped in deep water is easy. You can bail and sponge, or invert the boat and "throw" it free. However, *climbing back aboard* in running waves, is another matter! In rough water, you'll probably have to swim, so best be prepared for it!)

Recommended Reading

(Includes Information Unique To The Solo Canoe)

Basic River Canoeing, by McNair and Landry, American Camping Assn. 1985.
Canoeing Wild Rivers, by Cliff Jacobson, ICS Books, 1989.
Path of the Paddle, by Bill Mason, Van Nostrand Reinhold, 1980.
Tne New Wilderness Canoeing & Camping, by Cliff Jacobson, ICS Books, 1986.

7. SIT'N SWITCH CANOEING— THE RACER'S EDGE, by Harry Roberts

Harry Roberts, editor and co-founder of CanoeSport Journal, *has spent over 20 years promoting the gospel of fast cruising canoes and "sit'n switch" style paddling. He edited* Wilderness Camping *Magazine in the 70's, and has authored four books and hundreds of magazine articles. He came to the outdoor arena from a background of teaching high school and college literature, and, incongruously enough, engineering project management. He describes himself as "a professional writer and teacher, an amateur theologian and a cumpulsive talker." Harry is the asknowledged guru of "sit'n switch" canoeing, or "North American Touring Technique," as it's sometimes called. (CJ)*

Preliminary Splash

The circle is still unbroken. I was Cliff Jacobson's first editor, back in the palmy days of *Wilderness Camping* magazine in the 70's. And now he's my editor for this book. But—be warned. After 15 years or so, we still don't agree on a lot of technical items about paddling. So, what you read here may differ from what Cliff suggests.

Who's right? Both of us. What I tell you will work. What Cliff tells you will work. Why, if either approach will get you across the lake, around the portage and down the river easily and efficiently, do we disagree?

Some of the difference is a matter of style. I like to paddle aggressively and then stop and gawk at the scenery aggressively. Cliff prefers a gentler, steadier pace, and gawks as he goes.

37

Some of the difference is boat preference. Cliff likes the "all-rounder" that combines decent maneuverability and decent efficiency. I prefer the hot touring solo that runs very easily—and can be a handful to turn.

The result is that we've each chosen a paddling style that optimizes what we like to do on a tour, and is tuned to match the canoes we prefer. The style I've chosen is called North American Touring Technique (NATT), or "sit-and-switch". It's derived from the technique used by marathon racers throughout North America, and it's conceded to be the most efficient and most easily learned of all the paddling techniques. Here's how it's done.

The Basics of NATT

The NATT paddler *sits* in the canoe, usually on a contoured bucket seat. The paddler's feet rest against foot braces to provide additional leverage. The paddle is a bent-shaft of 10 to 14 degrees. The paddler switches sides to assist in keeping the canoe going straight, and makes all turning and sideslipping maneuvers from the "power" side. In other words, a right turn is made from a right hand paddling position; a sideslip to the left is made from a left hand paddling position. *You don't use cross-over strokes in NATT.* You don't use a pry stroke, although you may use a modified pry called a *pushaway*. And you don't use an exaggerated correction at the end of the power stroke to maintain direction. You use a slight correction, and switch sides regularly. This maintains speed and equalizes the wear and tear on your body.

The Strokes

You only have to learn three basic strokes; the *power stroke*, the *post*, and the post's active relative, the *draw*. It's useful to add a fourth stroke, the *pushaway*, to your repertoire if you like to paddle in constricted waterways, because you might not have room to switch sides and draw to move the boat sideways. In terms of classical paddling, with its complex correction strokes and crossover strokes, NATT is simplicity itself. But there's a catch. You must be able to do all these strokes from either side with equal or near equal facility.

Paddle sizing is important. If the shaft of your paddle is too long or too short, you'll be working from a biomechanically inefficient position, and you'll be losing the inherent efficiency of NATT. How to size the paddle? Sit erect on a flat bench. Turn the paddle upside-

Figure 7-1,2,3. Sit'n switch—the power stroke

down, with the handle on the bench. Your nose should come to the throat of the inverted paddle, that place where the shaft blends into the blade. Blade width? Eight inches; less if you can find it.

Hand spacing is important too. If you stand erect, with your arms hanging naturally at your side, and grasp the paddle, you'll find that the hand nearest the blade (your "bottom" hand) is about 2'1/2 hands' width above the blade. That's your most efficient hand spacing. If your bottom hand is closer to the paddle's throat than this, you sacrifice reach on the power stroke, and you're forced to lean with each stroke, which makes the canoe turn in the direction you don't want it to go.

The power stroke (figure 7-1, 7-2, 7-3) is done with your arms away from your body and nearly straight. It's no different than the stroke Cliff has shown you in Chapter 5, but the bent shaft paddle will give you a longer reach forward. Rotate your upper body slightly as you swing the paddle forward. Do NOT lean forward to make the catch. "Hinging" at the waist puts you in a very inefficient, very uncomfortable position. Stay erect; start the stroke from your feet, and feel the power flow through your whole body. Now—STOP the stroke as your upper body rotates back to "square". The power phase of the stroke ends just before the paddle *blade* is perpendicular to the water. You're not "pulling" with your arms. They exist mainly to connect your body to the paddle. Once the paddle blade catches the water, it's okay to lean against the paddle. In fact, if you think about driving the blade tip *down*, you'll get a better stroke. Just don't pull back with your arms.

Just as the power stroke ends, push the thumb of your grip hand (your "top" hand) away from you, as if you were unscrewing the top of a pickle jar. Lift the paddle out of the water, with your arms in the same position as they were, rotate, and take another stroke. That little twist of the top hand provides a slight correction that helps to keep the touring solo on course. It's not as exaggerated as a J-stroke; it's more like what Canadian paddling texts call a "pitch" stroke.

After a few strokes—three to six, usually—the canoe will start to wander off course, drifting away from the side on which it's being paddled. Switch sides, and keep paddling. Here's how.

The switch is easy to master, but it does require some practice. The secret is to never let go of the paddle. Let's start on our right side. As you take the paddle out of the water in a normal recovery, let your right hand slide up the paddle shaft to the grip as you release your left hand from the grip and grasp the shaft with it. Play with this maneuver on dry land for a few minutes, and you'll start to get it. In time, you'll be able to switch sides at 60 strokes a minute and not miss a stroke! For now, though, be clean, be positive. After a half-hour on a lake, you'll have switched sides enough to make a clean, quick switch and go directly into a draw stroke to move the canoe away from a rock. And you'll just get better and better at it as you paddle.

Figure 7-4. Post: "Get up speed, lean away from the turn...and 'post'."

The post (Figure 7-4) is a static draw stroke, and it's used to carve a moderate turn with very little loss of speed. For a *right* turn, do this: switch to your right side if you're not there already; place the paddle in the water somewhere between your knees and your hips, with the power face of the blade opened at about 30 degrees and the shaft vertical. It's almost like placing a power stroke, except the blade face is open and you're not rotating your body to drive the boat forward. If the boat is moving at a moderate pace, it will turn to the right.

NOW...if you lean to the opposite side, keeping your shoulders over your hips and using the force of the water flowing against the opened paddle face to help you feel secure, the canoe will turn faster because you've reduced the pressure on the stems. To turn *right*, then, post *right* and lean *left*. Don't lean to the right with the post; the blade isn't oriented to brace against. You'll note that this puts you in a position to go immediately into a power stroke.

If you place the *post* in at your side (rotate your upper body to face the paddle), the canoe will slip sideways and will not turn. If you need to move sideways faster, use the draw.

The *draw* (see page 25) will move the boat sideways with more power. In a sense, it's a forward stroke done perpendicular to the keel line, rather than parallel. Rotate your upper body, place the paddle in the water well outboard and forward of your hip, blade immersed and parallel to the keel line and shaft vertical, simply take a "forward" stroke, turning the thumb of your grip hand away from you at the end of the stroke and slicing the blade back through the water for another draw if you need it. (Note that an NATT style *draw* requires an *underwater recovery—CJ*.)

Your "top" hand is outboard of the rails, right? Try this with the boat at rest until you get the hang of it. And, of course, try it from both sides. Most people goof by stabbing at the water rather than maintaining a smooth flow of power. It takes time to master the draw. But you need to know how to do it right.

The *pushaway* (figure 7-5) is somewhere between a draw done in reverse and a wimpy pry. It's not a powerful stroke, but it will move the canoe sideways to your off (non-paddling) side enough to miss an obstruction in a situation where there isn't enough room on your off side to switch sides and draw or (horrors!) do a crossdraw. If you like to paddle blackwater rivers and swamps—and I do—you'll learn the pushaway. Here's how.

Figure 7-5. Pushaway.

The blade is fully immersed next to your hip, with the paddle shaft "oververtical", both hands outboard of the rails, with your grip hand farther outboard than your "bottom" hand, and your upper body rotated to face your work. The blade is parallel to the keel line, or slightly closed. Now, just push the paddle away from the canoe, using your body to push through against your "bottom" arm. Try this with the boat at rest and then with the boat moving. Once you're comfortable with it from both sides, try slicing the paddle through the water in a forward arc at the end of the stroke, so you can link the pushaway to a power stroke.

These, then, are the strokes that make NATT different from all other styles, and more efficient. Certain other strokes that Cliff has outlined in chapter 5 will be be useful parts of your repertoire. The *sculling draw* is handy for moving away from the shore in shallow water. The *reverse sweep* to a *bow draw* is a useful combination of strokes if you need to pivot the boat and head back to where you came from with some alacrity. And a *reversing stroke* is always useful.

Is NATT Just For Flatwater?

That's the myth. NATT and bent shaft paddles, so say the folks who've never learned to master them, can't be used in whitewater. The truth is that *all* downriver open canoe racers paddle NATT, with bent shafts. Granted, they're just blowing through the rapids, and not playing in them, but touring paddlers don't play either. And they're not paddling in severe whitewater. Not with gear in their boat; no way! That's what portage trails are there for!

Remember that a solo boat designed for NATT paddlers may not be a desirable boat in whitewater, because it's typically low-volume and relatively straight-keeled. It doesn't turn easily, and while it rises excellently to lake waves, it tends to submarine in aerated water. Yes; paddlers with good skills can run this breed of canoe in Class II whitewater (easy rapids with waves up to three feet high) comfortably, and in bigger Class III if they're very good and very selective, but that's not what these canoes were made to do. That paddlers can use these boats in such conditions should indicate to you that NATT is a powerful paddling style that enables you to move a boat from side to side easily—and for most touring paddling, the ability to move sideways is at least as important as the ability to make tight turns.

Concluding Splash

Paddling is a pleasure and a joy. The object of technical skill in paddling is not to impress your friends; it's to become one with your boat, the paddle, the water and the air. Skill is liberating. You simply do what you have to do, without thought, and let the whole wide, wild world flow through you. Love the wind. Embrace the wave. Delight in the precise move. Savor the sweat. Be one with sister osprey and brother hawk. Glory in the turtle. Caress the rock.

8. THE ELEGANCE OF FREESTYLE
by Charlie Wilson

Charlie Wilson is a flatland farmer with a paddling fetish. He introduced high-tech pack design to canoesport in the early eighties with his manufacturing company, GRADE VI, and is responsible for numerous innovative design concepts in touring luggage for paddlers.   .

Charlie organizes CONCLAVE, a national series of industry-wide, on water, paddling events. A dedicated advocate of "Sport" or "Freestyle" paddling, he seems determined to convince the nation that canoes should be smaller, lighter, more responsive, and tipped to their beam rails to be enjoyed.

A frequent industry consultant on both canoe and paddle design, Charlie writes about equipment and Freestyle paddling technique for several canoeing periodicals, serves as Sport Solo editor for Canoesport Journal, *and is finishing a book, FREESTYLE PADDLING, with Lou Glaros (CJ).*

The Freestyle Canoe

"Freestyle", or sport solo canoes differ from their touring bretheren in two ways: they are relatively smaller—both shorter and more slender—which results in a somewhat slower but more energy-efficient hull. They also have an above water shape with enough volume to lift the canoe's stems clear of the water when the boat is heeled to either beam rail. These factors combine to produce a craft that responds to your wishes NOW!

Because sport canoes are less than rock-stable when you sit in them, they are best paddled from a secure kneeling position. Pushing down on the left knee while lifting the right, leans the craft securely to port (and vice-versa)—that is, as long as your belt buckle stays inboard of the lower knee. It's okay to sit with legs outstretched when touring calm water (especially with a stabilizing load of gear on board), but to wring the most from your craft, you'll *kneel* with your knees wide-spread against the bilges.

Why on earth would anyone want to lean a canoe off-center when paddling it? For better control, and to make more effective turns, of course! Most solo canoes are designed to run straight when kept on an even keel, but they turn best when leaned substantially.

Rolling a canoe down to its beam rail drastically changes its in-water shape. The center line is now the curved chine of the hull; the stems (ends) of the boat are out of the water, which shortens the waterline length. Thus, by smartly heeling right or left, you can change a lean, straight-keeled touring hull into a radically rockered playboat! A strong lean allows you to more easily move (with your paddle) the bow or stern into a new position. With enough velocity, you can pull the bow to one side, thus encouraging the stern to skid around it for a faster turn.

When heeling the canoe right or left, hold your upper torso upright and control the "roll" of the hull with your lower body. Over-the-rail leans, as seen in exhibition freestyle events, are showy but insecure, and constitute poor form. Imagine a pin running down your spine. Keep it pointed towards the center of the earth and you'll be fine.

Hold the paddle loosely enough in your hands so you can rotate it to progressively open the power-face of the blade as a turn slows. This isn't easy if you have a death-grip on the grip or shaft.

It's neat to knee steer through a riffle, your paddle across the rails, but when you combine strong leans with linked paddle strokes to perform a maneuver, the interaction of hull, paddle, water and mind, come together in a pleasing whole of elegant movement.

Shift Your Weight for Better Control!
You can further alter the performance of your canoe by shifting your weight forward or aft. Leaning forward buries the bow and encourages the unweighted stern to whip sideways in an accelerating skid. Aft weighting (lean back) allows the bow to be drawn sideways more easily while keeping the stern on track.

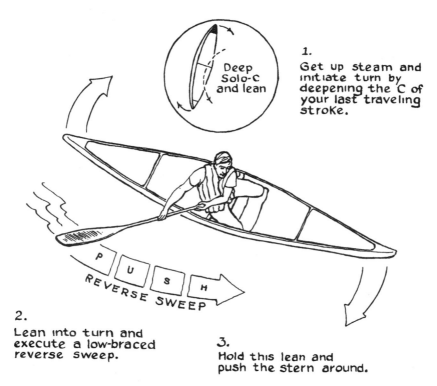

Figure 8-2. The Snap Turn

Learn to Paddle on *Both* Sides of Your Canoe!

Part of the freestyle game is to exert *precise* control over the canoe *without* having to change paddle sides to complete a maneuver. However, when touring, you'll occasionally switch sides to reduce fatigue and/or to make more effective turns. So practice all maneuvers on *both* sides of your canoe.

Maneuvers

The Snap Turn (Figure 8-2)

Here's a snappy way to turn towards your paddle side. Get up some steam, then initiate the turn by deepening the C of your last traveling stroke, leaning the hull towards your paddle to free the stems. As you complete the C, heel the boat deeper into the turn while rotating the paddle onto its backface, the leading edge lifted, so that the paddle planes across the water. Now, hold the lean and push the stern around the turn with a low-braced *reverse sweep*. The trick is to extend the duration of the rotational force, not maximize it in a short power burst.

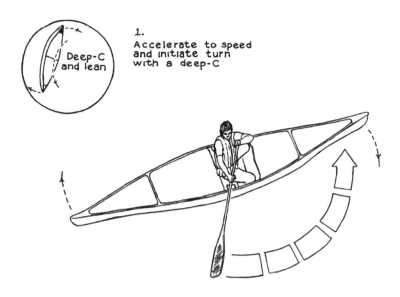

1.
Accelerate to speed
and initiate turn
with a deep-C

Deep-C
and lean

2.
Lean towards the paddle and plant a high brace
with the paddle face open about 45 degrees.
If satisfied with the turn, carry the high brace
forward and blend to another traveling stroke.

Figure 8-3. Onside Axle

This turn should carry you past 90 degrees, but will leave you dead in the water as linear momentum is transfered to the stern's skid.

On-side Axle (Figure 8-3)

The "on-side axle"—an inside leaned skid around a *hanging draw* (high brace)—preserves more momentum than the *snap turn*.

Accelerate to speed then initiate the axle with a deep C on your "On" or paddle side. Now, take the paddle out of the water and plant a knuckles-up *high brace* with the paddle's power-face open at 45 degrees to the keel-line while heeling the paddleside rail down to the water. The canoe should carve a tightening arc around your paddle. The *on-side axle* is quicker than a *snap turn* because you draw the bow towards the paddle, allowing momentum to skid the stern around. It has the additional advantage that you can carry the *high brace* forward and smoothly draw into your next traveling (Solo-C) stroke as you heel the boat upright.

The "Post"

So far, you've been leaning your canoe *towards* the turns. Now, try heeling *away* from the turn. An off-side heel increases the speed of the turn by adding hull deflection to the equation. This maneuver, called a *post*, concludes in an even more radical skid. Harry Roberts has described it for you on page 41.

Use the post when you want to make a secure turn without losing much hull speed. It's a great way to pop into an eddy from a *gentle* current. Caution: you must quickly heel the canoe back the other way (up river) as soon as you cross the eddyline. A strong up-current lean can provide an upsetting experience!

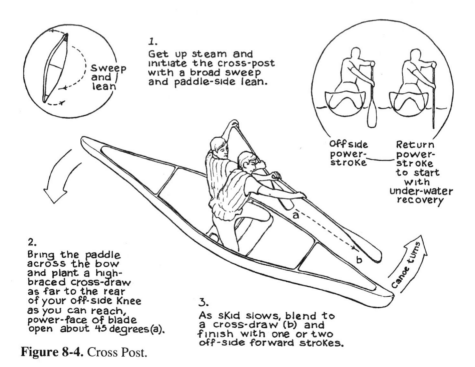

1.
Get up steam and initiate the cross-post with a broad sweep and paddle-side lean.

Sweep and lean

Offside power-stroke — Return power-stroke to start with under-water recovery

2.
Bring the paddle across the bow and plant a high-braced cross-draw as far to the rear of your off-side knee as you can reach, power-face of blade open about 45 degrees (a).

3.
As skid slows, blend to a cross-draw (b) and finish with one or two off-side forward strokes.

Canoe turns

Figure 8-4. Cross Post.

The Cross-post (Figure 8-4)

So far, you've been making all turns towards your paddle side. Suppose you want to turn the other way. You could flop the blade across the hull and switch hands, or simply *cross draw*. These procedures will work, but they are unspectacular. Better to use a *cross post*.

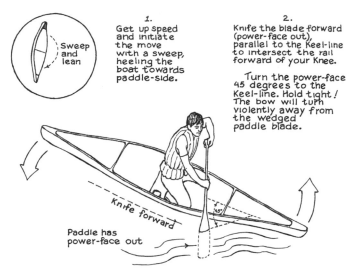

Figure 8-5. Bow Wedge

Get up steam and initiate the maneuver with a broad sweep. Drop your paddleside knee (lean *towards* your paddle) as you complete the *sweep*, to carve the bow of the canoe *away* from the paddle. Carry recovery of the paddle across the bow (turn your torso smartly) and plant a high-braced cross-draw as far to the rear of the off-side knee as you can reach, the power-face open about 45 degrees to the keel line. *Don't* change top hands! Essentially, the stroke is a near-vertical stationary cross-draw, applied as far behind your body as you can reach.

Now...drop your outside knee till the rail is wet and ride the turn out. As the skid slows, slip the paddle forward, opening the power-face a bit to keep the skid going; but the trick is to have patience enough to *let the boat make the turn*. When you've turned far enough, blend to a conventional *cross-draw* and into one or two *off-side* forward (power) strokes before retrieving the paddle to your on-side. Nifty! Now, try it again with the rail right down to the duckweed.

The Bow Wedge (Figure 8-5)

To make a more radical skid towards your off-side, use a *bow wedge*. Get the hull moving forward and initiate the move with a *sweep*, heeling the hull down towards your paddle side with your on-side knee.

As you recover the paddle from the initiating *sweep*, emphasize a forward weight shift as you knife the blade forward, power-face *out* to intersect the rail at a 45 degree angle, *forward* of your knee. Now, hold the paddle shaft tight against the rail. The bow of your canoe will turn violantly away from the blade as the outward-heeled stern planes around the bow in a radically accelerating skid.

Note: because you may be using a bent-shaft paddle, or one with a committed power face, you must *always* rotate the shaft so that the power-face of the blade is *outside* (not inside) the wedge.

Procedure: as you complete the *sweep*, rotate the shaft forward 90 degrees with your top hand, then slide the paddle ahead and wedge it against the hull. This orientation allows you to complete the turn with a sweep...or if things get out-of-hand, a high brace.

Bent or Straight Paddle?

"Bents" are more effective than straight blades when wedged with the power-face out. The angled blade lays nicely along the hull's vee. Conversely, they are markedly less efficient when used with the power-face in. That's why you need to turn them around when you execute a "wedge".

Linked Strokes

The *wedge* is an unbraced, intermediate quietwater maneuver. It doesn't require the linking of different strokes that characterize advanced moves. Let's combine a few every day strokes to make some advanced freestyle turns.

The Christie (Figure 8-6)

An advanced version of the low-braced *snap turn*, the *christie* has a critical wrinkle—the palm roll, which links the deep solo-C stroke to the low-braced reverse sweep. This maintains the same power-face through the turn, significantly increasing the integrity of the brace, and allowing continuity of rotational force, so you can skid a greater angle of turn with the same power.

Initiate the turn with a deep solo-C, heeling the canoe towards your paddle as the blade passes under the hull. (It is important that the top hand be outboard of the lower hand for a solo-C to be effective.) When you've reached the corrective portion of the C, and have rotated your top hand's thumb outwards and down (see CJ's description of this stroke on page 22), loosen your grip and start pushing the blade

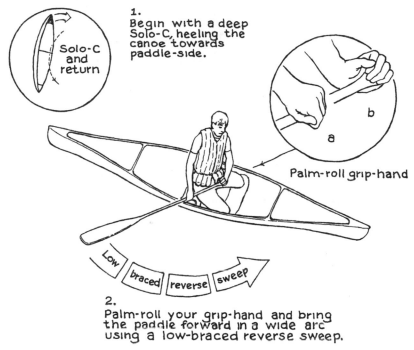

1.
Begin with a deep Solo-C, heeling the canoe towards paddle-side.

Solo-C and return

Palm-roll grip-hand

Low braced reverse sweep

2.
Palm-roll your grip-hand and bring the paddle forward in a wide arc using a low-braced reverse sweep.

Figure 8-6. The Christie

outwards. The outward movement of the vertical paddle blade will stabilize the paddle enough so that the top hand can slip (be "palm-rolled") 180 degrees around the grip. Remember to maintain inward pressure in the top grip with your thumb while the first and second finger roll around the grip, and your fingers when the thumb slips around.

The rolled top hand rotates the blade over to a proper, knuckles down, low brace—sweep angle flat enough to provide plenty of bracing downforce, the leading edge lifted so it won't dive into the water. The strong bracing action of this move allows you to securely heel the boat, rails awash, without capsizing.

The Christie works fine with a straight paddle, but it really shines with a 14-degree bent-shaft. It's even more effective with a large-bladed touring bent-paddle. With the blade almost flat on the water, you can lift the front edge more, and gain increased rotational force. Think about how ineffective a brace would be if you used the back-face of a bent paddle. Better yet, try it!

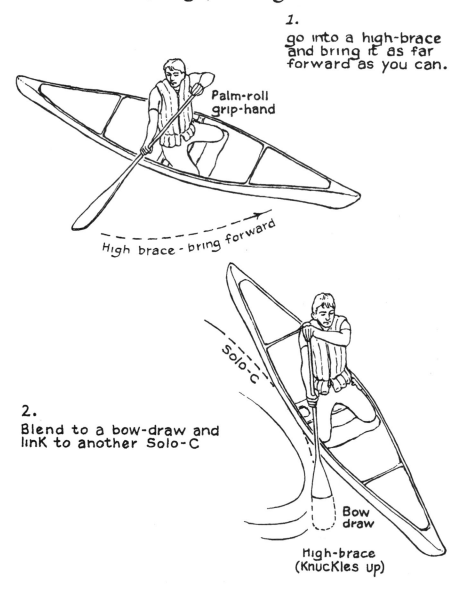

When canoe has skidded past 90 degrees in a Christie move, palm-roll your grip-hand again and...

1.

go into a high-brace and bring it as far forward as you can.

Palm-roll grip-hand

High brace - bring forward

2.
Blend to a bow-draw and link to another Solo-C

Solo-C

Bow draw

High-brace (Knuckles up)

Figure 8-7. Reverse Combination

Reverse Combination – Inside Pivot

The Christie is a classy move, but a low-braced *reverse-sweep* looses effectiveness as it comes abeam—when you've skidded past 90 degrees. What to do? Try another palm-roll—this time, to a knuckles-up, *high brace.*

Begin by lifting your top hand as you bring the blade through the *reverse sweep.* When the blade is abeam, your top grip should be almost throat high, with the top hand continuing to provide upwards force and the lower hand still pulling inwards on the paddle shaft.

Maintain your lean and continue the *high brace* forward as far as you can reach, coming off your seat to enhance forward weighting. Blend the brace to a *bow draw* and link this to another deep *solo-C* to complete the turn. Or, you can palm-roll off the C to another Christie and link to another *high brace* and around again, effectively screwing yourself into the swamp 180 degrees at a crank.

We call this maneuver the *Reverse Combination* or *Inside Pivot.* It's the best choice when you *really* have to make that turn and want a secure brace all the way through. It's lots of fun to practice on the pond, where 180 degree turns are practical. Once you've mastered it forwards, try the maneuver in reverse. Now, you're in for some fun! But that's another story and it should be told in another book.

9. SOLO CANOES AND CAMPING TRIPS

There's a notion that solo cruising canoes are too small, too slow, too fragile, and too unseaworthy for extended wilderness travel. A day or three on a quiet stream, or a week in the Boundary Waters or Quetico, is fine. But tackle a wild Canadian river for half a month? You've got to be kidding!

Concerns are well-founded. After all, the typical solo canoe is a scant foot deep and barely more than twice as wide. To this, add a relatively flat sheerline, minimal rocker, and concave, current-grabbing stems (ends), and you have all the makings of a whitewater submarine, even when running empty with just a swim-suited paddler aboard.

Room for tripping gear? Minimal! Solo canoes are too wind-susceptible to stack equipment above the rails as is the rule when tandem touring. So you've got to be creative: a narrow, tapered packsack fore and aft, maybe a thwart bag or two—that's all. You learn to pack light.

Luggage

A narrow, medium-sized packsack of around 3,000 cubic inch capacity (Charlie Wilson's impeccable GRADE VI bag is perfect for this application) and a standard size nylon day pack is all you need for trips up to two weeks. For longer excursions, you'll need another day pack.

Figure 9-1. Solo canoes and camping trips.

Place sleeping gear, clothes, tent and rain tarp in the large pack, which loaded, should weigh under 45 pounds. Stow this unit, belly side down, under a thwart, in the forward or aft section of your canoe. The day pack contains food and kitchen furnishings, pile pullover and rain-gear, gloves, fire-making tools and sundries—in all, maybe 25 pounds. A thwart bag on your seat frame holds drinking cup, sunglasses and bug dope.

Stow the day pack and wood yoke (three pounds) in the opposite compartment of your canoe and adjust trim by moving these items back and forth. No need to break the waterproof seal on your big tripping pack to get a rain coat, hat or sweater: these items are in your day pack.

Portaging the Load

Here's where the two pack system really shines. First, roll your front splash cover forward and reef it just behind the deck plate. Install your yoke and begin the carry in this order:

First trip over the portage, carry your big tripping pack, both paddles and camera (50 pounds). Second trip, bring the light day pack and canoe (around 55 pounds, depending on canoe weight). If you carry a second day pack (three pack system) on lengthy trips, try this arrangement:

1. Carry the big pack and the lightest day pack first. I always use a tumpline, even on the GRADE VI, so the little pack rides effortlessly overhead. Carrying a bulky pack across your chest as advised by some authorities, is dangerous where the footing is unsure. You must be able to see your feet as you plod along the portage trail!

2. Second trip, bring the heavy day pack and canoe. In no case should either load be over 60 pounds.

The Rapids

When dancing horsetails loom ahead, it's time to snap down your splash cover and batten all hatches. I grab my long straight paddle and shove the bent-shaft under the front cover, pushing the paddle forward until the blade wedges between the cover and deck (or rails, as the case may be). This produces a taut ridge-pole which effectively sheds water. If necessary, I can grab the spare paddle by reaching through the elasticised cockpit hole.

Equipment Concerns

If you're traveling in the company of friends, you can split the weight and bulk of community items like tent, stove, kitchen fly, axe, saw and cooking gear. But if you're going alone, you'll have to manage it all. Here's how I reduce the size and weight of my solo kit:

Tent: Most tents have poles which are too long to fit crossways in a medium size tripping pack. The Cannondale Aroostook, with its 18-inch pole sections, is the exception. One solution, is to lash long poles (in a nylon bag) to a thwart so they won't be lost in a capsize.

You can save carrying a two pound cooking tarp by converting your double-walled tent to a rainfly. Just attach quick-release Fastex buckles to the nylon webbing or shock-cord which secures the tent body to the fly corners. When rains come, unsnap the tent from the staked fly at any two adjacent corners, push the canopy aside, and cook your meal on the ground, under the fly.

On lengthy solo trips, I eliminate my precious handaxe, but not my wood-framed *Fast Bucksaw*. My fixed blade knife is substantial enough to split light kindling for a fire. Though I own a half dozen trail stoves, I invariably go with an old Primus 71 or MSR Whisperlite.

Cookware consists of a 2 1/2 cup stainless tea kettle and a liter size aluminum Sigg pot with cover that doubles as a plate. These, plus a Sierra cup, an insulated mug and spoon, are enough for a week.

Scenario: You're cruising along when a thunderstorm begins. Rain comes down in thick sheets as visibility approaches zero. Even with your splash cover on, you are not having a good time. Besides, it's high noon and your stomach is growling: might as well put ashore and kill some time till this thing blows over.

Almost any level spot along the shoreline will do. First, unsnap one side of your splash cover from the canoe then invert the boat and prop it overhead (shove the bow over a low tree limb). Push the draped cover outward with a few sticks or your paddles to create a narrow fabric umbrella. Now, use your pack for a backrest and fire up the stove. Some hot soup will re-warm your spirits until the storm subsides.

Granted, you've got to give up some comforts to canoe the backcountry alone in a pure-bred solo canoe. But you can sleep as late as you like, travel as fast or slow as you wish, eat when you want, stop at or bypass every swimming hole, laze for hours in the afternoon sun, or establish a base camp and do nothing at all. Solo canoes allow you to please yourself without compromising your ways for anyone.

10. YACHTSMANSHIP

My friend Bob Brown once eyed my three impeccably maintained solo canoes and suggested that I was really a yachtsman at heart. "Canoes should show some battle scars," says Bob: "Shows you're a canoeist not a canoer!"

In the event you disagree, here are some tricks that will keep your solo canoe looking and performing like new.

Maintenance of brightwork: oiled wood rails are easier to maintain and more flexible (less likely to break in a wrap-up) than varnished ones. Strip away varnish and rub in Watco Marine oil. A small amount of walnut stain added to the oil will darken wood to a pleasing glow.

To restore gray, weathered woodwork, sand well, then apply trisodium phosphate (TSP) cleaner, available at hardware stores. Work in with a stiff brush and wear protective gloves. Rinse completely, allow to dry, then sand to silky smoothness. Afterwards, rub in more Watco oil.

After each trip, pour a little Watco on a rag and go once over the rails. Wipe off the excess with a clean cotton rag. Once each season, cut the oil to the surface of the wood with 400 grit wet sandpaper and resume the oiling process. Your woodwork will develop a deep, rich patina.

Storage: store your canoe upside down, on carpeted saw horses, *in the shade*. If you must store your canoe outside, provide a rain/shade cover for it. *Do not* allow the cover to contact the canoe: rot and/or color-fading will result.

Water will accumulate under the decks and rails of inverted wood-trimmed canoes and cause rot and separation. For this reason, some solo canoes are constructed without confining deck plates. A small drain hole drilled just under the apex of the deck will let water out and is nearly invisible.

Hull maintenance: Use a commercial hull cleaner (I've had good results with *Star brite*) to remove scum lines and stains from fiberglass gel-coat. Paste wax will brighten and protect the hull but it will also increase resistance (wax is hydrophobic) to the water.

Gel-coat repair kits are difficult to use and never produce a good color match. Instead, fill gouges with white marine polyester putty (all marinas have it). Sand flush and polish with 400 grit wet sand paper. Spray paint with matching auto acrylic, then blend the paint to the surrounding area with fiberglass rubbing compound. Down time on the boat is less than an hour and the repair is unnoticieable.

Metal fittings loosen over time. Tighten them at least twice a season. Wood dents caused by over-tight screws may be (filled with clear epoxy, sanded flush.

High quality solo canoes *appreciate* over time: preventive maintenance goes a long way towards preserving your investment.

APPENDIX 1

SOME COMMON SOLO CANOEING TERMS

abeam: just off the side of the canoe.

beam: the widest part of the canoe.

beam rail: the point on the gunnel which represents the widest part of the canoe.

bent paddle: a paddle with a blade that is off-set 2 1/2 to 15 degrees. Also called "angle paddle".

freestyle: balletic style of sport canoeing. Paddlers kneel and use relatively straight paddles. They never switch sides to maneuver!

gel coat: the shiny outer skin (resin) of a fiberglass/Kevlar canoe. Gel-coat scratches and chips when you hit rocks.

gunnel (gunwales): the upper rails of a canoe.

heel: to lean the canoe.

hogged: a canoe with a bent-in keel line. The opposite of "rocker".

inwale: that part of the gunnel that is inside the canoe.

keel line: the center line of the canoe, from stem to stern. Good solo canoes don't have keels. Period!

NATT: North American Touring Technique (also called "sit'n switch). The canoeist sits on a form-fitted seat and powers the canoe with a short bent-shaft paddle, switching sides as needed to stay on course.

off-side: the side of the canoe opposite to that on which you're paddling.

oil can: denotes a canoe bottom which flexes in the water. Try this test: bounce on the seat. If the canoe bottom ripples (oil cans), performance is reduced. Some flexibility is desirable in a whitewater canoe, but not in a fast tourer.

on-side: the side of the canoe on which you are paddling.

outwale: that part of the gunnel which is outside the canoe.

palm roll: when you rotate the palm of your hand around the grip of the paddle to expose the opposite face of the blade to the water.

rocker: the upward curve of the keel line of the canoe.

s-blade: high performance freestyle paddle whose blade is shaped in a lazy S.

saddle: a foam or plastic kneeling pedestal—a characteristic of whitewater and freestyle canoes.

sit' n switch: same as NATT

slider: slang for "sliding seat".

stem (s): the extreme ends of a canoe. Some stems are straight; others are gently curved or (traditionally) recurved.–

tender: a canoe which feels unstable (tippy) at rest.–

tracking: the ability of a canoe to stay on course without constant correction. Also refers to hauling a canoe upstream with the aid of "tracking lines".

yoke: the removeable, padded thwart with which you carry your solo canoe.

INDEX

Upgrade Your Outdoor Skills . . . Read The
Basic Essentials Series

- Includes Bookland EAN/UPC codes
- Abundantly illustrated
- 72 pages each
- Only $4.95 each

each only $4⁹⁵

Other books by Cliff Jacobson

The Basic Essentials Series

Map & Compass
Get off the most commonly traveled paths and streams far away from the intrusion of other people in your search for wilderness and solitude. Relocate a favorite fishing spot or portage and find your way back to your car using a simple road map. Update out-of-date maps.
ISBN 0-934802-42-4 $4.95 U.S. $6.95 Canada

Camping
Cliff continues his efforts to increase the skill level of the general camping public. Of course, a thorough explanation of gear is concisely included for campers interested in procuring equipment. Fire starting procedures and camp cooking are discussed in detail. Finding a lack of basic skills in camps everywhere, Cliff devotes a chapter to "ropemanship." Map and compass skills are another area effectively covered in this book.
ISBN 0-934802-38-6 $4.95 U.S. $6.95 Canada

Knots in the Outdoors
Windproof your tent and rain fly with expert knots. Tie off your watercraft with knots you can depend on. Cinch down cargo while traveling to your destination. Splice ropes together when necessary. Includes a left-hand mirror image illustration of every right handed knot and hitch.
ISBN 0-934802-57-2 $4.95 U.S. $6.95 Canada

Cooking in the Outdoors
His unique ideas and sensible solutions to typical campsite dilemmas will make food stay edible longer and taste better. Plan meals for groups. Bake bread and cookies using a variety of portable ovens. Prepare freeze-dried foods. Cook in the rain. Obtain safe drinking water. Dispose of wastes properly. Protect food from bears. Sometimes considered the most difficult and burdensome part of a camping trip; cooking responsibilities encompasses meal planning, food procurement and disposal concerns.
ISBN 0-934802-46-7 $4.95 U.S. $6.95 Canada

Canoeing
Cliff again sets his goals to increase the skill level of paddlers. As a professional guide, he believes what "beginning canoeists need most is an easy-to-read text which tells, without beating around the bush, the important things that are essential to safe, enjoyable canoeing." Cliff's ideas are original. He offers some unique canoeing techniques and custom design tips never released.
ISBN 0-934802-39-4 $4.95 U.S. $6.95 Canada

Titles beyond the basics...

Canoeing Wild Rivers
Expanded by more than 50 pages and revised with over 200 updates, Canoeing Wild Rivers remains what OUTDOOR ALASKA recommends as "the first book you should obtain." With input from leading experts and anecdotal accounts to color the contents, Cliff covers everything to include covers, carriers, salvage, portaging and transportation.
ISBN 0-934802-52-1 $19.95 U.S. $26.95 Canada

Camping Secrets
SHHH! don't let the experts know what Cliff has done. He's divulging treasured secrets, kept hidden for decades. Different from other camping books, it has alphabetical listings for quick reference access. Cliff also reveals some unique advice on how to rig a rain trap, and how to build a dependable fire. Gain the advantage on camping friends with advice from an expert.